Most Remarkable Writers

Jayn Arnold • Glen Downey

Series Editor
Jeffrey D. Wilhelm

Much thought, debate, and research went into choosing and ranking the 10 items in each book in this series. We realize that everyone has his or her own opinion of what is most significant, revolutionary, amazing, deadly, and so on. As you read, you may agree with our choices, or you may be surprised — and that's the way it should be!

an imprint of

www.scholastic.com/librarypublishing

A Rubicon book published in association with Scholastic Inc.

Rubicon © 2008 Rubicon Publishing Inc.
www.rubiconpublishing.com

All rights reserved. No part of this publication may be reproduced, stored in a database or retrieval system, distributed, or transmitted in any form or by any means, electronic, mechanical, photocopying, recording, or otherwise, without the prior written permission of Rubicon Publishing Inc.

 is a trademark of The 10 Books

SCHOLASTIC and associated logos and designs are trademarks and/or registered trademarks of Scholastic Inc.

Associate Publishers: Kim Koh, Miriam Bardswich
Project Editor: Amy Land
Editor: Christine Boocock
Creative Director: Jennifer Drew
Project Manager/Designer: Jeanette MacLean
Graphic Designer: Sherwin Flores

The publisher gratefully acknowledges the following for permission to reprint copyrighted material in this book.

Every reasonable effort has been made to trace the owners of copyrighted material and to make due acknowledgment. Any errors or omissions drawn to our attention will be gladly rectified in future editions.

"Harry Potter and the Sad, Empty Feeling" (excerpt) by Rebecca Dube, July 12, 2007. Reprinted with permission from *The Globe and Mail*.

"11th Century Japan: The Tale of Genji" (excerpt). Transcript from Books & Writing, "11th century Japan: The Tale of Genji" first published by ABC Online, January 19, 2003, is reproduced by permission of the Australian Broadcasting Corporation and ABC Online. © 2003 ABC. All rights reserved.

"I'm nobody! Who are you?" Reprinted by permission of the publishers and the Trustees of Amherst College from THE POEMS OF EMILY DICKINSON: READING EDITION, Ralph W. Franklin, ed., Cambridge, Mass: The Belknap Press of Harvard University Press. Copyright © 1998, 1999 by the President and the Fellows of Harvard College. Copyright © 1951, 1955, 1979, 1983 by the President and Fellows of Harvard College.

Cover image: J. K. Rowling–Photo by Eamonn McCormack/WireImage

Library and Archives Canada Cataloguing in Publication

Arnold, Jayn
    The 10 most remarkable writers / Jayn Arnold, Glen Downey.

ISBN 978-1-55448-553-6

    1. Readers (Elementary). 2. Readers—Authors. I. Downey, Glen R., 1969- II. Title. III. Title: Ten most remarkable writers.

PE1117.A76 2007   428.6   C2007-906861-8

1 2 3 4 5 6 7 8 9 10   10   17 16 15 14 13 12 11 10 09 08

Printed in Singapore

Contents

Introduction: Accomplished Authors 4

J. K. Rowling 6
Rowling has sold over 350 million copies of her books worldwide!

Murasaki Shikibu 10
A 10th-century author, Shikibu wrote *The Tale of Genji* — the first novel in the history of literature.

Lewis Carroll 14
Among his many other remarkable accomplishments, the author of *Alice's Adventures in Wonderland* is credited with popularizing nonsense fiction.

Theodor Seuss Geisel 18
With his humorous rhyming stories and whimsical drawings, "Dr. Seuss" has captured the imaginations of generations of readers.

Charles Dickens 22
Victorian England comes to life in the pages of Dickens's famous novels.

Ralph Ellison 26
Ellison's *Invisible Man* is considered one of the most important books of the 20th century!

Jane Austen 30
Austen's ability to write about universal human emotions has made her books relevant even today — nearly 200 years after they were written!

J. R. R. Tolkien 34
Hobbits, Ents, and Orcs first came to life in Tolkien's incredible epic fantasies.

Emily Dickinson 38
An innovative writer who revolutionized poetry, Emily Dickinson is regarded as one of America's greatest poets.

William Shakespeare 42
He isn't known as "The Bard" for nothing! Shakespeare wrote some of the most impressive works in the history of literature.

We Thought 46
What Do You Think? 47
Index 48

ACCOMPLISHED AUTHORS

Don't tell me the moon is shining; show me the glint of light on broken glass.
— Anton Chekhov

Writing something fabulous is as easy as putting pen to paper, right? Not quite! It takes more than a pen and a piece of paper to write a memorable and groundbreaking work. Great writing is unique and imaginative. It tells a captivating story or captures a vivid mood. It connects with readers, no matter where they are from or what their age. Throughout history, there have been many amazing and accomplished writers. The writers featured here have wowed readers with their poetry, plays, novels, and short stories. Some are master storytellers. Others describe the world in such detail that readers feel immersed in their works. These great writers are also good researchers. Their works are intelligent and artistic. Many of these writers wrote their greatest works centuries ago — and they're still hugely popular today!

In this book, we present our choice of the 10 most remarkable writers. We selected and ranked them using these criteria: the extent to which their writings have touched and inspired readers; their talent at writing; their influence on other writers; the length of time their works have endured; the number of copies their books have sold — around the world and in different languages; and the awards they have won.

Turn the pages and read about these 10 remarkable writers. As you do so, ask yourself the following question:

vivid: *intense; bright; full of life*

WHO IS THE MOST REMARKABLE WRITER OF ALL TIME?

10 J. K. ROWLING

J. K. Rowling is shown here after being honored with the highest degree from Edinburgh University, Scotland, in 2004.

A WRITER IS BORN: Born on July 31, 1965, Joanne, aka J. K., Rowling rose to fame in 1997 after the publication of *Harry Potter and the Philosopher's Stone*.

LITERARY LOCALE: Rowling lives and writes at her homes in England and Scotland.

THE WRITE STUFF: Rowling was a teacher and aspiring writer before the Harry Potter series made her a billionaire and one of the world's most successful authors.

It's hard to believe, but there was a time when people didn't know what a Muggle was! Up until 1997, people didn't even know how Quidditch was played! Today, it's hard to imagine a world without Harry Potter. J. K. Rowling's books are "with the exception of [certain] religious and political tracts … the bestselling books of all time," according to *Globe and Mail* columnist Kate Taylor. Readers love Rowling's imaginative writing. Each book is filled with action-packed story lines. These coming-of-age stories set in a magical world appeal to readers of all ages!

Before the Potter series catapulted her to stardom, Rowling was an unknown. She was struggling to get by — working part-time jobs and collecting welfare. However, she was also working on her first novel. It took her four years to complete the book. Finally, in 1997, *Harry Potter and the Philosopher's Stone* was published. The publisher initially printed only 500 copies of the book — it didn't take long for them to sell out!

Rowling has written seven Harry Potter books. Many of these have been made into hit Hollywood movies. Rowling is famous worldwide. Kids all over the globe now have a renewed interest in reading, thanks to the Potter books. For her remarkable contribution to popular fiction, Rowling ranks #10.

---

tracts: *short literary works*
coming-of-age: *about reaching maturity; becoming an adult*

J. K. ROWLING

THAT'S REMARKABLE!

In her Harry Potter series, Rowling created a remarkable fictional world. Magical creatures and plants, such as Hippogriffs and the Whomping Willow, are common sights. Rowling's books are "fast-paced and humorous, with page-turning plots that are essentially teen-detective stories," according to writer Kate Taylor. This has given the books widespread appeal. They offer young readers an escape from the everyday world. Even adults enjoy them!

> **?** Is it fair to consider a writer remarkable because he or she has sold a lot of books? Why or why not?

Quick Fact
The last book in the series, *Harry Potter and the Deathly Hallows*, sold more than 10 million copies in its first weekend. In total, more than 350 million copies of the Potter books have been sold worldwide!

FAMOUS FIGURES

Living among the pages of the Harry Potter books are wizards, witches, and Muggles. Muggles, or regular people, are completely unaware of the magic surrounding them. Harry Potter is the young wizard after whom the series is named. Orphaned as a baby, Potter is raised by Muggle relatives. On his 11th birthday, he discovers his hidden talents — wizardry! Ron Weasley and Hermione Granger are Potter's pals at Hogwarts School of Witchcraft and Wizardry. In charge of the school is Albus Dumbledore — a man considered the best wizard of his generation. Lord Voldemort, or "He-Who-Must-Not-Be-Named," is the evil wizard who terrorizes Potter and his friends.

STILL GOING STRONG

The boy wizard's future looks uncertain. In July 2007, *Harry Potter and the Deathly Hallows* was released. This is the seventh, and supposedly final, book in the series. But just before releasing the book, Rowling said "never say never," when asked whether she would write another Potter novel. At the very least, fans can look forward to seeing the last two books come alive on the big screen. And in 2009, truly enthusiastic fans will be able to step inside Potter's world! A Florida theme park called "The Wizarding World of Harry Potter" will bring locations such as Hogwarts, Hogsmeade, and the Forbidden Forest to life!

> **?** Have you read any of the Harry Potter books? If so, what, in your opinion, makes Rowling a remarkable writer?

Kids dressed up as their favorite Harry Potter characters wait in line to get the latest book.

The Expert Says...

" [The Potter books have] made millions of kids smarter, more sensitive. ... I don't know of any books that have worked that kind of magic on so many millions of readers in so short a time. ... "

— James Thomas, Department of English, Pepperdine University, California

Harry Potter and the Sad, Empty Feeling

A newspaper article from *The Globe and Mail*
By Rebecca Dube, July 12, 2007

As the wildly successful series nears its end, fans fret about what they'll do once they've read the final page. …

Regardless of who lives or dies in *Harry Potter and the Deathly Hallows*, fans who have grown up with the boy wizard … will be mourning the end of an era. …

The books may be make-believe, but post-Potter depression will be quite real for some fans. …

Mourning the end of a beloved book or series is a normal rite of passage. … [But] in this case the literary loss is shared by an unusually large number of people. …

Emptiness, depression, and even anger are among the emotions Harry Potter fans expect to feel when they turn the final page. …

For some, the series will never really be over.

"Look at *Star Trek* fans — they're still going strong 40 years after the series ended," Ms. Mitchell [a Ph.D. candidate in late medieval literature at Duke University] says. "Do I think we're going to see the end of Harry Potter fandom? Not at all."

rite of passage: *experience that marks a change from one stage of life to the next*

Quick Fact
Rowling was very involved in how her books were adapted into movies. She insisted that the main actors be English and that the movies be filmed in the United Kingdom.

Take Note
Rowling's impressive accomplishments put her at #10. The Harry Potter books have sold an incredible number of copies. They have been made into popular films and have earned Rowling billions of dollars. The books have also inspired a whole generation to see literature as a source of inspiration and entertainment. Rowling's stories appeal to readers of all ages and each book has been as successful as the last.
- Rowling's books were written fairly recently. Do you think this should disqualify her from being included on a list of the 10 most remarkable writers? Explain.

9 MURASAKI

In this painting by Japanese artist Tsukioka Yoshitoshi, author Murasaki Shikibu is seen looking out from the veranda of a monastery on a moonlit night.

SHIKIBU

A WRITER IS BORN: Murasaki Shikibu (A.D. 973–1014) was born in Japan.

LITERARY LOCALE: Shikibu lived during Japan's Heian period, which lasted from A.D. 794 to 1185. This period was known for its amazing art and literature.

THE WRITE STUFF: Shikibu is remembered mostly for her remarkable work, *The Tale of Genji*. This book is considered by many to be the first novel in the history of literature.

Centuries before the earliest Western novels were written, a young Japanese woman was writing *The Tale of Genji*. Though nobody knows the author's real name, she came to be known as Murasaki Shikibu — a nickname based on one of the famous characters she created. Shikibu's classic story of love and intrigue still appeals to readers today, centuries after it was written.

As a young woman, Shikibu was sent to live at Japan's imperial court. She worked as a lady-in-waiting, or attendant, to the empress. Shikibu wrote stories to entertain the ladies of the court. Together, these stories became *The Tale of Genji*. This work is divided into 54 sections. Each section depicts a series of episodes in the life of the central character. *The Tale of Genji* is twice as long as Leo Tolstoy's *War and Peace* — a novel with more than 1,400 pages! Shikibu's novel takes place in a very engaging setting. The main character goes through moments of great happiness. Just like in real life, however, there is also personal misfortune.

Shikibu lived so long ago that little is known about her life. What is known is that she had a great talent for writing. *The Tale of Genji* continues to encourage readers to lose themselves in a fantastic fictional world.

---

intrigue: *suspense; mystery*

MURASAKI SHIKIBU

Quick Fact
A talent for reading and writing ran in Shikibu's family. Her daughter also grew up to be an accomplished writer.

THAT'S REMARKABLE!

The Tale of Genji "may well be the first novel ever written," according to Royall Tyler, who translated the work. But that's not the only amazing thing about this piece of literature! *The Tale of Genji* has more than 400 characters. It follows four generations of one family. The book is also considered the world's first psychological novel. A psychological novel looks deep inside the minds of its characters. This book doesn't just tell a story. The author explores the feelings and motivations of each character's actions throughout the work.

STILL GOING STRONG

It's been almost 1,000 years since Shikibu wrote *The Tale of Genji*. To this day, readers continue to be amazed by the work's wealth of detail. "Many things about the lives of the characters … are of course unfamiliar now," says Royall Tyler. "[But] their feelings, motives, and experiences are recognizable to anyone." The work's fame has never been surpassed in Japan. *The Tale of Genji* is still "one of the longest and most distinguished masterpieces of Japanese literature," according to the *Encyclopedia of World Biography*.

FAMOUS FIGURES

The main character in *The Tale of Genji* is Hikaru Genji. He is Shikibu's most famous character. Hikaru is the son of a Japanese emperor. Since his mother is not from a noble family, he is raised as a commoner. The story follows his journey to adulthood. As he discovers who his parents really are, he also finds out things about himself. Hikaru Genji is a fool for love! His many relationships allow him to experience a full range of emotions — from exhilarating joy to crushing sorrow.

? Shikibu's literary reputation is based largely on a single work. Do you think an author should have written more than one famous work to qualify as remarkable? Explain.

The Expert Says…

> *The Tale of Genji* … is the highest **pinnacle** of Japanese literature. Even down to our day there has not been a piece of fiction to compare with it.

— Yasunari Kawabata, Japanese writer and winner of the Nobel Prize in Literature

pinnacle: *highest point or level*

An artist's rendition of Murasaki Shikibu's *The Tale of Genji*

11th Century Japan: THE TALE OF GENJI

In this radio interview, translator Royall Tyler talks to Ramona Koval of the Australian Broadcasting Company about Murasaki Shikibu.

January 19, 2003

Ramona Koval: … Royall Tyler is a scholar of Japanese language and literature. …

Royall Tyler: *The Tale of Genji* is right up there with the great classics of world literature. … I cannot understand what genius it must have taken to write *The Tale of Genji*. It's extraordinary. Nobody came anywhere near it, ever again.

RK: What do we know about Murasaki Shikibu? …

RT: We know a little, but not very much. She was probably born in approximately 973. She was the daughter of a provincial governor. … So Murasaki Shikibu belonged to a middle level of the aristocracy which, in the capital, supplied ladies-in-waiting to the greatest lords and ladies around the emperor. …

RK: A woman who wrote. Was this unusual in her time? She would have been unusual in Western culture.

RT: No, it wasn't by Murasaki Shikibu's time. The official written language at the court was Chinese, even though the courtiers of the time did not speak it. These courtiers — men — studied history, philosophy, and religious texts in Chinese, and also wrote poetry in that language … the women wrote in Japanese. …

aristocracy: class of people holding a high rank or social position

Take Note

Murasaki Shikibu takes the #9 spot. Rowling's books made her a billionaire. However, we think it's more remarkable that Shikibu's single novel has endured for 1,000 years and is still being read.
• Do you agree with the author's ranking? Explain.

3   2   1

8 LEWIS CARR

A portrait of Lewis Carroll, 1863

OLL

A WRITER IS BORN: Charles Lutwidge Dodgson (1832–1898), aka Lewis Carroll, was born in England. In 1865, Carroll published *Alice's Adventures in Wonderland*.

LITERARY LOCALE: Carroll lived and worked in Oxford, England.

THE WRITE STUFF: Carroll wrote two of the most famous works in the history of children's literature. He also introduced the world to "nonsense fiction."

"**O**h dear! Oh dear! I shall be late!" There's nothing strange about these words, except for the fact that they are being spoken by a rabbit! And not just any rabbit, but one wearing a vest and reading a watch! Welcome to a world where nothing makes sense, everything seems upside down, and anything is possible. This enchanting storybook setting is the backdrop to Lewis Carroll's *Alice's Adventures in Wonderland*. Not only was the book hugely popular, it also made Carroll famous.

Before he shot to fame, Carroll was a math professor. He worked at Oxford University in England. However, writing was Carroll's real passion. He started out writing books based on math theory and logic. He also published several articles, poems, and short stories in magazines. When Carroll made the jump from numbers to novels, his unique writing style really caught people's attention! His books, *Alice's Adventures in Wonderland* and *Through the Looking-Glass*, are two of the cornerstones of children's literature.

In his books, Carroll looked at language in an innovative way. He mastered the art of writing books for kids that also appealed to adults.

cornerstones: *foundations; most important parts*

LEWIS CARROLL

 Lewis Carroll and J. K. Rowling both wrote books for children. Why do you think Carroll ranks higher? Do you agree with this ranking? Explain.

THAT'S REMARKABLE!

Carroll had a unique, somewhat scientific understanding of language. This allowed him to bend the traditional way people used language. For example, Carroll created something called portmanteau (port-man-toh) words. These are words formed by combining the sound and meaning of two words into one. "Smog," from smoke and fog, and "brunch," from breakfast and lunch, are good examples. Carroll invented new words to show how anything was possible in wonderland. For him, "mimsy" was a mix of flimsy and miserable. "Slithy" was a combination of slimy and lithe. Carroll was also a master of satire. Through his imaginative and appealing stories, he shared his views on the strengths and weaknesses of 19th-century English society.

STILL GOING STRONG

Carroll's works of nonsense fiction have become a part of Western popular culture. The Alice books are his most famous works, but Carroll wrote other novels. He wrote amazing nonsense poems like "The Hunting of the Snark" and "Jabberwocky." Several movies and TV shows, cartoons, and songs are based on Carroll's works. Many writers have been inspired by Carroll's innovative writing style. There's even a medical condition called "Alice in Wonderland Syndrome." People with this syndrome see things bigger or smaller than they really are.

FAMOUS FIGURES

Carroll's famous protagonist, Alice, was named after Alice Liddell. She was one of Henry Liddell's daughters. He was the dean of the school where Carroll taught. Carroll entertained Alice and her sisters by telling them fantasy stories. Soon, he was inspired to write down his enchanting tales. The Mad Hatter, Tweedledum and Tweedledee, and the Cheshire Cat are just a few of Carroll's other clever creations.

lithe: *flexible; lean*
satire: *wit or humor used to attack or expose people's weaknesses*
protagonist: *main character*

Quick Fact
Charles Lutwidge Dodgson used a pen name to protect his privacy. To come up with his pen name, he translated Charles Lutwidge into Latin. This gave him the name Ludovicus Carolus. He then loosely translated this back into English to get Lewis Carroll.

pen name: *name that an author uses in place of his or her real name*

The Expert Says...
" The clue to the enduring fascination and greatness of the Alice books … lies in language. [Its] endless intriguing puzzles continue to reveal themselves long after we have ceased to be children. "
— A. S. Byatt, author

Nonsense 101
Get to know the Jabberwock!

Learn more about nonsense fiction in this article.

Lewis Carroll popularized a type of writing called nonsense fiction. However, this name is slightly misleading. "Nonsense" writing actually makes sense. It just makes sense according to a different set of rules. Take a look at the following excerpt from a poem found in Carroll's *Through the Looking-Glass*. The poem called "Jabberwocky" includes many invented words. These words don't seem to make any sense at all! When you read the poem, though, you get a pretty clear idea of what is happening. The poem tells the story of a boy who slays a dangerous beast. This poem is thought to be one of the most remarkable works of nonsense fiction ever written.

… "Beware the Jabberwock, my son!
The jaws that bite, the claws that catch!
Beware the Jubjub bird, and shun
The frumious Bandersnatch!"

He took his vorpal sword in hand:
Long time the manxome foe he sought —
So rested he by the Tumtum tree,
And stood awhile in thought.

And as in uffish thought he stood,
The Jabberwock, with eyes of flame,
Came whiffling through the tulgey wood,
And burbled as it came!

One, two! One, two! And through and through
The vorpal blade went snicker-snack!
He left it dead, and with its head
He went galumphing back. …

Quick Fact
In 1998, a first edition copy of *Alice's Adventures in Wonderland* broke the record for the most money ever paid for a children's book at auction. It sold for $1.5 million dollars!

Take Note
Children's author Lewis Carroll ranks #8. As brilliant as her novel is, Murasaki Shikibu is not as famous as Carroll. Carroll produced more works than Shikibu. His works have also reached a wider audience. Carroll remains remarkable because of his originality.
• What do you think of nonsense fiction? Give reasons why Carroll's innovative way of writing impresses, or doesn't impress, you.

7 THEODOR SEU

Author Theodor Geisel is surrounded by some of his most famous characters on this 2004 commemorative U.S. postage stamp.

SS GEISEL

A WRITER IS BORN: Theodor Seuss Geisel (1904–1991), aka Dr. Seuss, was born in Springfield, Massachusetts.

LITERARY LOCALE: Geisel first became famous in New York City but eventually settled in California.

THE WRITE STUFF: Geisel combined his remarkable artistic talent with his gift for rhyme and produced some of the most memorable children's books of all time.

Theodor Geisel was not a real doctor but, using the pen name "Dr. Seuss," he made a lot of people feel better! Geisel grew up in Springfield, Massachusetts. When he was in his twenties, he enrolled in a Ph.D. program in English literature. However, soon after starting, Geisel changed his mind about finishing his degree. He moved to New York City to work as a cartoonist. In the 1930s, Geisel decided to combine his talent for drawing with his writing skills. He wanted to create a children's book. In the beginning, things didn't go too well. His first book, *And to Think That I Saw It on Mulberry Street*, was initially rejected by dozens of publishers. Geisel was told that his book was too different from other children's books on the market. Geisel didn't give up and eventually, one publisher decided to take a chance on his innovative style.

Geisel's stories were anything but traditional, which is probably why he experienced so much rejection at first. His unique tales featured imaginary places, people, and creatures. They were written more like poems than stories. Geisel used simple vocabulary so that even young children could understand and enjoy reading his stories.

The first Dr. Seuss book was published in 1937. After that, Geisel was "on his way to becoming America's most popular children's book author," according to the *New York Times*.

THEODOR SEUSS GEISEL

Quick Fact

Geisel won a Pulitzer Prize in 1984. He was honored "for his special contribution over nearly half a century to the education and enjoyment of America's children and their parents."

THAT'S REMARKABLE!

When Geisel was starting out, most kids were reading educational books known as "Dick and Jane" books. These books helped kids learn to read. But, "[m]any people found them boring," according to Ohio State University professor David Bloome. Dick and Jane books always featured the same characters. The writing was very repetitive — a few simple words were used over and over again. Geisel revolutionized books for young readers. He introduced "humorous, rhymed, and colorful books," according to the *St. James Encyclopedia of Pop Culture*. Geisel's books have helped generations of kids improve their reading skills. The simple tales have also taught kids important life lessons. *The Lorax,* for example, teaches the importance of caring for the environment.

FAMOUS FIGURES

From the Grinch to the Cat in the Hat, Yertle the Turtle to the Lorax, Geisel created some unforgettable characters! The Grinch, from *How the Grinch Stole Christmas*, is one of Geisel's most famous creations. He's a grouch who sets out to ruin Christmas. However, along the way, the Grinch learns the true meaning of the holiday. In 2000, comedian Jim Carrey starred in *The Grinch*, a Hollywood movie based on Geisel's book. The Cat in the Hat, from Geisel's 1957 book of the same name, is Geisel's other most famous figure.

STILL GOING STRONG

Geisel believed that children want the same things as adults, "to laugh, to be challenged, to be entertained, and delighted." Maybe this explains why his books appeal to both children and their parents! Geisel's whacky, **whimsical** stories and drawings are popular around the world. Hundreds of millions of copies of Geisel's books have been sold. The number of children's TV specials and feature length films based on Geisel's work are proof of his lasting legacy.

whimsical: *fanciful; unusual*

Quick Fact

In 2004, the U.S. Postal Service issued a commemorative stamp to mark the 100th anniversary of Geisel's birth. On March 11, 2004, Geisel was also honored with a star on Hollywood's Walk of Fame.

? Why do you think the writings of J. K. Rowling, Lewis Carroll, and Dr. Seuss are so popular with children and adults?

Geisel is hard at work on drawings for How the Grinch Stole Christmas.

PROTECTING THE ENVIRONMENT
ONE VERSE AT A TIME

Each one of Theodor Geisel's books teaches an important lesson. Read this **article** and see how his book *The Lorax* spread environmental awareness.

The Lorax was first published in 1971. It is one of Geisel's famous **allegories**. It tells the story of a character named the Once-ler. After arriving in a new town, the Once-ler decides to go into business. He starts cutting down Truffula trees and turning them into a garment called a thneed.

Soon the Lorax appears. As he says, he "speaks for the trees." The Lorax asks the Once-ler to stop cutting down trees. But business is booming, and the Once-ler is greedy. He destroys more and more of the Truffula forest. It's not until the environment is devastated and his business fails that the Once-ler realizes he has done wrong.

This book teaches kids to respect and protect the natural world. "Long before saving the earth became a global concern ... [Geisel] warned against mindless progress and the danger it posed to the earth's natural beauty," according to his publisher Random House.

More than 35 years later, *The Lorax* still speaks to us about important issues. Theodor Geisel cared about our planet. Through his remarkable works, he has taught generations of kids to care about it as well.

allegories: *symbolic stories in which characters or places represent ideas or principles*

The Expert Says...

"The **alliteration** ... the stretching of the dictionary like bubble gum ... are Seussian traits that give our children an early taste for language, for flair, for the advantages of sounding smart ..."

— Tunku Varadarajan, professor at New York University

alliteration: *repeating of the same initial sound of words in a phrase or sentence*

Take Note

Geisel grabs the #7 spot. Both Carroll and Geisel wrote imaginative, memorable works for children that also appeal to adults. However, Geisel's books have helped millions of children learn to read. They are some of the most popular, creative, and enduring children's books ever written.

- There's a moral to each of Geisel's stories. Choose one of his books and explain what you think it teaches.

6 CHARLES DIC

Charles Dickens, seen here in 1849

KENS

A WRITER IS BORN: Charles John Huffman Dickens (1812–1870) was born in Portsmouth, England.

LITERARY LOCALE: When Dickens was 10 years old, his family moved to London. He lived and worked there the rest of his life.

THE WRITE STUFF: Dickens wrote an impressive number of novels. He populated them with some of the most amazing and memorable literary characters of all time.

Have you ever been told that experience is the best teacher? Well, it certainly helped Charles Dickens! At the age of 12, Dickens was pulled out of school. His father had landed in prison for not paying his debts, and Dickens was sent to work in a factory to help pay them off. Doing menial labor for hours each day, Dickens probably didn't have great expectations for his future. But despite his humble beginnings, Dickens grew up to become the most popular writer of his age. His extraordinary tales about London and Victorian society were inspired by his experiences and the world he lived in.

Dickens was a master at combining fact and fiction. His gripping stories were often loosely based on real people, places, and situations. His works were relevant because they brought important social issues to light. Dickens also created some of the world's most famous literary characters — from David Copperfield and Tiny Tim, to Scrooge and Oliver Twist.

The famous literary critic Edmund Wilson once called Dickens "the greatest writer of his time." A humble childhood inspired Dickens to write some of the world's most impressive literary works.

menial: *lowly; requiring little skill or training*
Victorian: *period of Queen Victoria's reign, between 1837 and 1901*

CHARLES DICKENS

> ❓ *The Pickwick Papers* was first published in monthly installments for a newspaper. What do you think would be the challenges of writing in installments?

THAT'S REMARKABLE!

"[One] of the greatest revolutions in publishing came more than 150 years ago, from the pen of ... Charles Dickens," according to reporter Matthew Davis. Dickens had an innovative way of writing. He was an expert at drawing readers in with his comical, easy tone. Once readers were hooked, Dickens got to the real issues! He used his works as a way to discuss, and often criticize, the society in which he lived. Dickens's first novel, *The Pickwick Papers*, was published in 1837. He wrote 14 other novels during his lifetime. "[Dickens] brilliantly depicted Victorian London, fought for social reform, and created some of the most indelible characters that fiction has ever known," according to the Public Broadcasting Service (PBS).

social reform: *efforts to make society fairer for women, children, and the poor*
indelible: *unforgettable; memorable*

> ❓ Do you think Dickens's tough childhood inspired him to write about social reform? What kind of books do you think he would have written if he'd grown up wealthy?

FAMOUS FIGURES

Dickens loosely based many of his characters on people he knew. He mixed different elements of people's personalities to create fictional, but realistic, characters. Because of this, Dickens's characters are complex, emotional, and flawed — just like real people. These characters come from every walk of life. Scrooge, from *A Christmas Carol*, is one of Dickens's most memorable characters. Today, we use the word "scrooge" to describe a stingy, miserable person, just like the Scrooge in the story. This stingy, miserable man is saved by the ghosts of Christmas past, present, and future. This tale shows the dangers of being greedy, selfish, and self-absorbed. Oliver Twist is almost as famous. This poor orphan, who in the story falls in with a band of thieves, was Dickens's first child protagonist.

STILL GOING STRONG

Dickens's novels, characters, and vivid portraits of 19th-century London are as captivating today as they were in his day. He remains one of the most popular English authors ever. Dickens's novels have been made into numerous films and TV shows. Perhaps the greatest of these is the 1951 version of *A Christmas Carol* starring Alastair Sim as Scrooge. In 2007, a theme park named "Dickens World" opened in Chatham, England. At the park, visitors experience the sights, sounds, and smells of Dickens's London!

Alastair Sim as Scrooge in the 1951 film, A Christmas Carol

The Expert Says…

"[In his novels, Dickens] was eager to reveal the often shameful ways in which we behave, and to make careful judgments about how we might act with greater decency, generosity, and fairness to one another."

— Joel J. Brattin, professor, Worcester Polytechnic Institute

The Movie World of Dickens

Dickens was a master at bringing his characters to life! He gave detailed descriptions of people and places. Get to know some of Dickens's most famous creations in these fact cards.

Oliver Twist: In 1968, the musical *Oliver!*, based on Dickens's book *Oliver Twist*, was made into a movie. The great success of the stage show helped to make the movie a hit. The movie was nominated for 11 Academy Awards. It won five, including the award for Best Picture. In 2005, a new version of the movie made it to the silver screen.

A Christmas Carol: Many famous actors have played the part of cold and miserly Ebenezer Scrooge. An upcoming film will star Jim Carrey as the infamous penny-pincher. Even Miss Piggy and Kermit have starred in a version of this classic — *The Muppet Christmas Carol*.

Great Expectations: Three of Dickens's most memorable characters are Pip, Estella, and Abel Magwitch from *Great Expectations*. This book follows the poor, orphaned Pip as he grows up and falls in love with the rich and sophisticated Estella. Several TV and movie versions of the book have been filmed over the years. A famous 1989 mini-series starred actor Anthony Hopkins as the escaped convict Magwitch. This character becomes Pip's secret benefactor and helps him become a gentleman.

---

miserly: *greedy and stingy*
infamous: *being famous for something bad*
benefactor: *somebody who helps, especially with a gift of money*

Mark Lester stars as Oliver Twist in the 1968 movie Oliver!

Quick Fact
"Dickensian" is an adjective used to describe everything from harsh living conditions to jolly and friendly characters. It also refers to something that is full of twists and coincidences, like Dickens's famous plots!

Take Note
Dickens takes the #6 spot. He wrote some of the most beloved novels in English literature. His characters have not faded with the passage of time. More than 150 years after they were published, his books are still widely read and studied.
- Use the Internet or the library to find information about two famous Dickens characters not mentioned above. In your opinion, what makes these characters remarkable? Why have they remained so popular after so many years?

5 RALPH ELLISON

During his lifetime, Ellison held prestigious positions at many universities. He was also an exceptional jazz trumpeter, sculptor, and photographer!

A WRITER IS BORN: Ralph Ellison (1914–1994) was born in Oklahoma City, Oklahoma.

LITERARY LOCALE: Ellison left Oklahoma in 1933 to study music at the Tuskegee Institute in Alabama. He later moved to New York City.

THE WRITE STUFF: Ellison is known largely for a single work of literature — a novel called *Invisible Man*. In it, he captures what it means to be black in America.

Ralph Ellison was destined for greatness. He was named after Ralph Waldo Emerson, a famous American philosopher. He was also born in a place of possibilities. In 1907, Oklahoma became the 46th American state. Ellison was a descendant of formerly enslaved African Americans. But he was born in a state known for freedom. When he was born, the state was only seven years old. It was seen as a frontier. It was a place of opportunity. Ellison's parents moved there hoping to escape the prejudice of the South.

In 1933, Ellison moved to Alabama to study music. There, he truly felt other people's racism toward him for the first time. This and his other life experiences influenced his career. In his writing, Ellison explored the American experience.

In *Invisible Man*, Ellison wrote about alienation. He wrote about being African American, but also about the universal human experience. "Boiled down, his message was about being human, and lost and aghast," according to the *New York Times*. A book that speaks universal truths, *Invisible Man* has connected with readers for more than 50 years.

---

frontier: *region just beyond or at the edge of a settled area*
alienation: *state of feeling withdrawn or isolated from others*
aghast: *struck with overwhelming shock or amazement; filled with sudden fright or horror*

RALPH ELLISON

THAT'S REMARKABLE!

Ellison is mostly known as a novelist. He also wrote award-winning short stories, essays, and lectures. However, *Invisible Man* is his most famous work. As soon as it came out, *Invisible Man* was recognized as a powerful work of fiction. Ellison's main character was unlike most other African-American protagonists of the time. This character was educated and ambitious. He suffered because of other people's prejudice towards him, but he didn't let this keep him down. Thanks to Ellison's innovative approach, *Invisible Man* "remains one of the most important novels about race and the lives of black Americans ever written," according to the *New York Times*. However, it also has universal appeal. As writer Roger Rosenblatt once said, "Ralph Ellison taught me what it is to be an American."

> *Invisible Man* is about being an outsider and being ignored. Do you think that people of all races and ages can relate to these feelings? How does it help to know that others feel the same way?

FAMOUS FIGURES

The unnamed main character and narrator of *Invisible Man* is Ellison's most famous figure. This character isn't actually invisible. "I am a man of substance, of flesh and bone, fiber and liquids," he says in the book's prologue. "I am invisible, understand, simply because people refuse to see me." In the book, the narrator travels across the U.S. He "becomes involved in an amazing series of adventures," according to publisher Random House. "[H]e is sometimes befriended but more often deceived and betrayed." Each experience helps the character grow. As he discovers things about himself and about his society, Ellison's hero enlightens readers about their own lives.

> Ellison's reputation is largely based on a single novel. Would you rather write one great novel or many good ones? Explain.

STILL GOING STRONG

In 1953, Ellison won the National Book Award for fiction for *Invisible Man*. He was the first African American to win this award. In 1998, *Invisible Man* came in at #19 on Random House Modern Library's list of the 100 Best Novels of the 20th century. In 2005, *TIME* magazine named *Invisible Man* one of the 100 best English-language novels written since 1923. *Invisible Man* is a classic work of American literature. It is required reading in many classrooms around the world.

enlightens: *informs; instructs*

On May 1, 2003, the "Invisible Man" sculpture was unveiled in Harlem, New York City, in honor of Ralph Ellison.

Quick Fact

Apart from *Invisible Man*, Ellison wrote three other major works. *Shadow and Act*, released in 1964, and *Going to the Territory*, published in 1986, are books of essays, reviews, and interviews. *Juneteenth*, a second novel, was finished by Ellison's editor and published in 1999 after Ellison's death.

Visible Praise for Invisible Man

Over the years, reviewers have had a lot of great things to say about *Invisible Man*. The following quotations will help you understand how people feel about Ralph Ellison's famous novel.

"[*Invisible Man* is] a book of the very first order, a superb book."
— Saul Bellow, Pulitzer Prize-winning author

"*Invisible Man* is tough, brutal and sensational … it blazes with authentic talent."
— Orville Prescott, *The New York Times*

"Ellison is a writer for all of us, black, white, and otherwise. He understands … the American experience, I think more deeply than anyone else that I have read."
— Charles Johnson, professor at the University of Washington and author of *Middle Passage*

"[*Invisible Man*] is the quintessential American picaresque of the 20th century."
— Lev Grossman, *TIME* magazine

quintessential: *most perfect example of something*
picaresque: *type of fiction in which the hero has many adventures*

Quick Fact
The year it was released, *Invisible Man* spent 16 weeks on the best-seller list!

The Expert Says…
" [Ellison] saw the predicament of blacks in America as a metaphor for the universal human challenge of finding a viable identity in a chaotic and sometimes indifferent world. "
— Anne Seidlitz, journalist

viable: *possible; reasonable*

Take Note
Ellison takes the #5 spot. He was a remarkably talented writer, musician, sculptor, photographer, and scholar. He also wrote one of the most important novels of the 20th century.
• *Invisible Man* is a coming-of-age story. Name some other coming-of-age stories you have heard about or read. What is it about this genre that really connects with people?

5 4 3 2 1

④ JANE AUSTEN

Jane Austen published her novels anonymously. This was standard practice for female writers at the time!

A WRITER IS BORN: Jane Austen (1775 – 1817), who wrote six of the most beloved novels in the English language, was born in the small town of Steventon, England.

LITERARY LOCALE: Austen lived her whole life in the English county of Hampshire.

THE WRITE STUFF: Austen wrote about ordinary, everyday events. By also focusing on human nature, she made her stories universally appealing.

You've probably heard of the popular movie *Bridget Jones's Diary*. What you might not know is that it was based on a book written by an author who lived in early 19th-century England. This woman was Jane Austen. She has inspired generations of readers with some of the most brilliant novels in the English language.

Austen wrote six complete novels before her death in 1817. She published her first novel, *Sense and Sensibility*, in 1811. *Pride and Prejudice*, *Mansfield Park*, and *Emma* followed. *Northanger Abbey* and *Persuasion*, Austen's last novels, were published after her death. All six of these works have been made into movies and adapted into television series. They have been modernized and retold. So, why are they still so popular? As author Tony Tanner once said, "[We] can still, despite the vast differences between her society and our own, recognize ourselves in the ways her characters think and behave."

In her novels, Austen explored the lives of middle- and upper-class men and women. She wrote detailed accounts of the communities in which they lived, worked, and socialized. Austen's original works are more famous today than they were when she was alive. She is recognized worldwide as one of history's most remarkable writers.

JANE AUSTEN

Quick Fact
In 2007, Austen's book *Pride and Prejudice* came in at #1 on a list of books that readers in England couldn't live without.

THAT'S REMARKABLE!
Austen had a profound understanding of people. In her books, she described in detail the ins and outs of daily life. She covered both the seriousness and humor of relationships. Austen understood what people were really thinking. She was also realistic when it came to romance. She acknowledged that economics and human flaws are factors in real-life love stories. Austen focused on the intimate details of the lives of her characters. She understood that people are more deeply affected by what is going on close to home than by things happening in other parts of the world.

> Austen has been criticized for keeping her focus too narrow. She rarely wrote about what was happening outside of her characters' lives. Can a writer still be great if he or she does not deal with important issues of the day? Explain.

FAMOUS FIGURES
Elizabeth Bennett is the heroine of *Pride and Prejudice*. She is an intelligent and practical woman. Unlike most people around her, she is unimpressed by wealth or social status. "I must confess that I think her as delightful a creature as ever appeared in print," Austen herself once said of Bennett. Mr. Darcy is another of Austen's most famous characters. He becomes Bennett's love interest despite the fact that the first time she meets him she thinks he's a snob! Austen's original title for *Pride and Prejudice* was *First Impressions*. One of the themes of the book is how first impressions can be deceiving.

> Jane Austen's novels were originally published anonymously. Why do you think this was the case?

STILL GOING STRONG
It's been nearly 200 years since Jane Austen wrote her novels. However, she continues to be a favorite among readers. Austen's books are reprinted and reissued every year. Hundreds of book, TV, and movie adaptations have been based on Austen's works. Remember Mark Darcy in *Bridget Jones's Diary*? He's based on Mr. Darcy from *Pride and Prejudice*. Just like him, many of Austen's characters have been used in new ways by modern writers. In recent years, there has also been renewed interest in Austen's personal life. Several biographies have been written about her. In 2007, she was also the subject of a movie called *Becoming Jane*.

In 2005, Keira Knightley played Elizabeth Bennett in a movie version of Pride and Prejudice. Knightley was nominated for an Oscar for her performance!

ALTERED AUSTEN

Jane Austen's works have been adapted in a number of interesting and creative ways. This list of contemporary works shows just how innovative some of the adaptations have been!

Clueless
(movie 1995)

This very successful film is based on Austen's *Emma*. This comic novel centers on a character named Emma Woodhouse. An intelligent but spoiled young woman, Woodhouse's favorite hobby is matchmaking! In *Clueless*, the story takes place at a Beverly Hills high school! The plot is similar to Austen's original, but Emma is replaced by a student named Cher Horowitz. Popular and fashion-forward, Horowitz makes it her goal to give the new girl in school a makeover and to find her a boyfriend ASAP!

Bridget Jones's Diary
(novel 1996, movie 2001)

This book was a huge success! A few years after it was published, it was made into a Hollywood movie. The story is a loose, modern-day retelling of *Pride and Prejudice*. Here, the main character is wacky and flawed. She falls for Mark Darcy, a character named after the hero in Austen's novel.

Bride and Prejudice
(movie 2004)

This is a Bollywood version of *Pride and Prejudice*. The movie follows the plot of Austen's work. However, it also has musical numbers and an Indian flavor!

Bollywood: *motion-picture industry of India, based in Mumbai (formerly Bombay)*

The Expert Says…

" Dead at 41, [Austen's] major phase lasted only six years. … Given another decade, she might have achieved an eminence that would startle even her most ardent admirers. "

— Harold Bloom, author and literary critic

eminence: *high ranking; reputation*
ardent: *passionate; eager; enthusiastic*

Take Note

- Jane Austen steps into the #4 spot. She wasn't known during her lifetime. It was after her death that her novels started to grab the public's attention. Austen based her works on her immediate surroundings. She had great insight into the subtle ways that people relate to each other.
- Thanks to the TV and movie versions of Austen's work, many people who have never read any of her books are familiar with her stories. What harm is there in experiencing an author's work only through movies or adaptations?

3 J. R. R. TOLK

J. R. R. Tolkien in his study, 1955

A WRITER IS BORN: John Ronald Reuel Tolkien (1892–1973) was born in South Africa.

LITERARY LOCALE: After serving in the army, Tolkien became a professor at Oxford University. It was here that he wrote his fantasy masterpieces.

THE WRITE STUFF: Tolkien's epic stories are incredible works of fantasy fiction. *TIME* magazine calls *The Lord of the Rings* the "founding text of modern fantasy literature."

It's a long way from Jane Austen's proper English society to Middle-earth, where elves, hobbits, and talking trees roam! Tolkien's Middle-earth is a fantastical world filled with heroes and legends. His works are now the standard against which all other works of fantasy are judged.

Tolkien worked as a professor for almost 40 years. When not teaching, he was busy working on his fantasy novels. Little did he know that these fantasies would become some of the most popular and respected books in English literature. *The Hobbit* and *The Lord of the Rings* trilogy are Tolkien's most famous works. His gripping stories and remarkable fictional universe have engaged and impressed readers for decades. His works present a dazzling array of characters, and offer breathtaking descriptions of otherworldly landscapes. Tolkien went so far as to invent new languages for some of his characters! He also drew detailed maps of Middle-earth.

Hugely imaginative and exciting, Tolkien's novels explore the conflict between good and evil. They also show the value of friendship, loyalty, and courage. An author known for fantasy fiction that educates and entertains, Tolkien is one-of-a-kind in the literary world.

---

trilogy: *series or group of three plays, novels, operas, etc.*

J. R. R. TOLKIEN

Quick Fact
It took Tolkien 14 years to complete *The Lord of the Rings* trilogy. This includes *The Fellowship of the Ring, The Two Towers,* and *The Return of the King.*

THAT'S REMARKABLE!
Tolkien was a brilliant scholar. He studied English literature and history. He was also familiar with Norse, or ancient Scandinavian, mythology. Knowledge of these time periods and legends had a huge influence on his writing. In his novels, Tolkien created an entire fictional universe. And, he didn't skimp on details! "By the time the reader has finished the trilogy … he knows as much about Tolkien's Middle-earth … [as] he knows about the actual world," according to poet W. H. Auden. Tolkien also invented a complete history to act as a backdrop for his stories. This allowed readers to fully understand Middle-earth's past.

 Tolkien has been applauded for his attention to detail. What challenges does an author of fantasy fiction face that authors of other genres might not encounter?

FAMOUS FIGURES
Among Tolkien's most famous characters are Frodo Baggins, Gandalf the Grey, and Gollum. Baggins is a young hobbit. In *The Lord of the Rings* trilogy he is faced with an enormous task. Baggins inherits the One Ring from his uncle Bilbo. He then finds out that to save Middle-earth he has to destroy the ring. To do this, he must throw it into the fires of Mount Doom! Gandalf the Grey is a powerful wizard. He helps Baggins in his quest. Gollum is one of Tolkien's most famous villains. He is a hobbit-like creature who used to own the One Ring. He is greedy, vicious, and dangerous, and he'll do anything to get the One Ring back!

STILL GOING STRONG
Every great fantasy writer since Tolkien's time is *indebted* to his amazing stories. He is considered by many to be the father of fantasy. Tolkien's works have also become a *staple* of popular culture. Recently, *The Lord of the Rings* trilogy was brought to life on screen. Three award-winning films based on the books were directed by Peter Jackson. The movies were a huge success. The final movie, *The Return of the King,* won 11 Oscar awards! It was the first fantasy film to ever win the Oscar for best picture. Thanks to the movies' popularity, Tolkien's books have found fame with a whole new generation of readers.

indebted: *obligated; owing gratitude*
staple: *essential element; necessary item*

 Fantasy is a genre that doesn't appeal to everyone. Why do you think this might be? Does it appeal to you? Explain why or why not.

Gollum is a famous villain from Tolkien's The Lord of the Rings.

The Lord of the Lists

Get a sense of Tolkien's fame in this **fact chart** *about his remarkable works.*

Solar Flare is a science fiction and fantasy news blog. In 2005, Tolkien took the #1 spot on the blog's list of the 10 Most Influential Fantasy Authors of all time. "Tolkien defines fantasy fiction," says the site's creator.

"Tolkienesque" is an adjective used to describe fantasy literature. A work that takes place in imaginary lands, has incredible, make-believe characters, and is about amazing adventures can be called Tolkienesque because it shares some of the qualities of Tolkien's works.

Together, Peter Jackson's three Tolkien movies were nominated for a total of 30 Oscars. They won a remarkable 17 awards! The trilogy earned more than $4 billion in box office revenues and sales of videos, soundtracks, and merchandise.

In 2003, *The Lord of the Rings* was chosen as the "Nation's Best-Loved Book" in a survey conducted in the United Kingdom.

The Lord of the Rings made *TIME* magazine's list of the 100 Best Novels from 1923 to the Present.

The Expert Says…

" Mr. Tolkien has succeeded more completely than any previous writer in this genre. … [N]o previous writer has … created an imaginary world and a **feigned** history in such detail. "

— W. H. Auden, poet

feigned: *fictitious; invented*

Take Note

Tolkien earns the #3 spot. His tales of Middle-earth have had a huge influence on popular culture. They also helped to define a genre and have greatly influenced other fantasy writers. Tolkien's detailed fantasy world is remarkable. His works are routinely listed as the greatest fantasy novels ever written.

- Tolkien drew maps and invented new languages for his books. How might this add to your enjoyment of a work of fiction? Explain.

5   4   **3**   2   1

② EMILY DICKI

Only two real photographs of Emily Dickinson exist. All other representations or images of her are based on these two photos.

NSON

A WRITER IS BORN: Emily Dickinson (1830–1886) was born in Amherst, Massachusetts.

LITERARY LOCALE: Dickinson never left her hometown. She led a relatively quiet life in her family's home in Amherst.

THE WRITE STUFF: Dickinson's poetry is completely original. In her poems she explores the themes of grief and isolation, as well as joy.

Emily Dickinson lived in relative seclusion in 19th-century New England. During her lifetime, Dickinson was considered an *eccentric*. She hardly ever left her house. She dressed all in white. She might have looked unusual and behaved in strange ways, but Emily Dickinson was a poetic genius. Though she wasn't famous during her lifetime, Dickinson's poems are now considered the cornerstone of American poetry.

Dickinson was a master at saying a great deal in very few words. Her poetry, like her, was unique and unconventional. Dickinson's poems were discovered in her bedroom shortly after her death, and were first published in 1890. At first, editors weren't sure how people would react to Dickinson's modern style. They "fixed" her grammar and altered the elements that made her writing unique. It wasn't until 1955 that Dickinson's poetry was finally published as she had originally written it. When people read her unedited poems, they were struck by Dickinson's originality, style, and talent. Dickinson's poetry was unlike anything people had ever read before!

Dickinson had one of the most original minds in the history of English literature. She wrote about 1,800 poems. Fewer than 10 of these were published before her death. These were all published anonymously. Dickinson never tasted fame. Today, however, she is known as one of the greatest poets to have ever lived.

eccentric: unusual, peculiar, or odd person

EMILY DICKINSON

THAT'S REMARKABLE!

In her poems, Dickinson was able to create a clear sense of suffering and passion. "[She] challenged the existing definitions of poetry and the poet's work," according to the Poetry Foundation. Dickinson was one of the first modernists. Modernist poets rejected traditional forms and themes. Dickinson used language, grammar, and expression in never-before-seen ways. She wrote in free verse. She used unusual dashes in her poems. She also capitalized words to make them stand out. These grammatical quirks give her poems emotion and energy.

? Dickinson was told by her friend Thomas Higginson that she shouldn't have her works published. What reasons can you think of for advising someone not to publish his or her work?

FAMOUS FIGURES

As a poet, Dickinson didn't use characters in the traditional sense. Because of this, it's the speakers in her poems who are her most famous figures. In Dickinson's poems, the speaker often recalls past happiness. The speaker also talks about the possibility for happiness in the future. The present, though, is usually seen as dark and lonely. "[The] speakers in Dickinson's poetry … are sharp-sighted observers," according to the Poetry Foundation. These speakers see "their imagined and imaginable escapes."

free verse: *poetry that doesn't follow a specific rhyme scheme or structure*

An oil painting of Emily Dickinson as a child

STILL GOING STRONG

During her lifetime, Dickinson was dismissed as an "untaught lady poet." Today, she is considered one of the pillars of American poetry. Her mysterious lifestyle has added to people's fascination with her. For years, scholars and critics have tried to understand why Dickinson withdrew from the world. They have also carefully studied her impressive works. When her poems were first published they were largely disliked, but modern audiences have embraced Dickinson's unique talent. Dickinson is credited with helping to define a truly American poetic voice.

Quick Fact
Dickinson wrote a lot of poems. In one year alone, she wrote 364 poems!

? Despite their talent, Emily Dickinson and Jane Austen were published anonymously. What does this tell you about attitudes toward women in the 18th and 19th centuries?

A Quiet Genius

During her lifetime, the quiet Emily Dickinson from Amherst, Massachusetts, kept much of her poetry hidden. After her death, she came to be regarded as one of the most original geniuses in the history of English literature. Here is one of her original poems.

I'm nobody! Who are you?

I'm nobody! Who are you?
Are you nobody, too?
Then there's a pair of us — don't tell!
They'd banish us, you know.

How dreary to be somebody!
How public, like a frog
To tell your name the livelong day
To an admiring bog!

The Expert Says...

"[Dickinson] is one of the most intelligent of poets and also one of the most fearless. If the fearlessness ran out, she had her courage."

— Galway Kinnell, Pulitzer Prize-winning poet

Take Note

For her amazing contributions to poetry, Dickinson ranks #2. Dickinson broke with tradition in her writing. By doing so, she helped define a uniquely American poetic voice. This has influenced generations of poets who came after her. Though she was never famous during her lifetime, Emily Dickinson is now considered one of America's most famous poets.

- Read some of Dickinson's poetry. See for yourself whether you like her works. Why do you think people have trouble understanding them?

2

1 WILLIAM SH

This statue of William Shakespeare stands in the Thomas Jefferson Building of the Library of Congress in Washington, D.C.

AKESPEARE

A WRITER IS BORN: William Shakespeare (1564 – 1616) was born in Stratford-upon-Avon, England.

LITERARY LOCALE: Shakespeare wrote most of his famous works in London.

THE WRITE STUFF: Shakespeare's poetry and plays have been the cornerstone of English literature for more than 400 years.

Ever heard of Romeo or Juliet? How about Hamlet or Macbeth? If so, then you have some knowledge of an incredibly talented writer called William Shakespeare. Through his timeless plays, Shakespeare brought these and many other characters to life.

Shakespeare is known as an outstanding playwright. He wrote hilarious comedies, heartbreaking tragedies, and moving dramas. And he is also one of history's most famous poets. Shakespeare wrote more than 150 sonnets. These poems, mostly about love, friendship, and beauty, are as meaningful and relevant today as when they were first written.

Shakespeare wrote more than 35 plays. Most of these are still regularly performed in theaters around the world. They are also required reading in most classrooms. Shakespeare's sonnets are just as famous. From romantic greeting cards to movie scripts, Shakespeare's words have been used in a wide range of places.

Shakespeare is world-renowned for his very significant contribution to literature. His works have crossed cultural boundaries. They have also proven to be timeless. This remarkable writer stands alone as history's greatest genius of fictional literature.

---

sonnets: *rhyming, 14-line poems, with 10 syllables in each line*

WILLIAM SHAKESPEARE

THAT'S REMARKABLE!

Shakespeare's themes are universal. His plays and poems deal with situations and emotions that most people experience at one time or another. "More than any other writer, he can teach us enormously about ourselves," says critic Harold Bloom. Shakespeare's characters fall in love and enjoy lasting friendships. They sometimes suffer pain and heartache, and sometimes feel guilty, betrayed, or confused. "[Shakespeare] had the uncanny ability to put into words what it means to be human," says *TIME* magazine writer Jumana Farouky.

> ? In adaptations, people often change the language or settings of Shakespeare's works. How might this affect an audience's appreciation of Shakespeare? Explain.

FAMOUS FIGURES

Almost everyone has heard of Romeo and Juliet. This ill-fated young couple has grabbed the imagination of generations of people through the play *Romeo and Juliet*, arguably Shakespeare's most popular. There is a ballet and an opera based on the play. Dozens of TV and movie adaptations of *Romeo and Juliet* have also been made over the years. Hamlet is another of Shakespeare's most well-known characters. The brooding, young prince is Shakespeare's most famous tragic hero.

uncanny: *beyond the norm; impossible*
tragic hero: *literary character who has a fatal flaw that brings on a tragedy*

Quick Fact
Shakespeare is often called simply "The Bard." Bard is another word for poet or writer.

STILL GOING STRONG

Shakespeare's popularity has endured the passage of time. His works continue to be praised by scholars and critics. He is recognized the world over as the most remarkable writer in history. "If Shakespeare stares out from the cover of a book, someone somewhere will buy it," says *TIME* writer Jumana Farouky. "[He's] a trusted brand." His plays are studied in school, and performed for enthusiastic audiences. There seems no end in sight to the Bard's popularity!

> ? Do you think Shakespeare's plays should be taught in schools? Give reasons to support your answer.

The Expert Says...

" Shakespeare is the only writer in world literature who actually comes close to belonging to the world. ... [H]is plays continue to be produced ... in many dozens of languages and countries. "

— Maynard Mack, author of *Everybody's Shakespeare*

Ethan Hawke starred as Hamlet in Michael Almereyda's 2000 movie version of Hamlet.

WHAT WOULD SHAKESPEARE SAY?

Shakespeare's words are profound and touching. Many of his sayings also sum up universal truths. Because of this, people have been quoting him for centuries. Check out these familiar Shakespeare **quotations**.

As You Like It

"All the world's a stage / And all the men and women merely players;"

In this line, Shakespeare suggests that life is like a play and that throughout life, people are just playing their parts.

Hamlet

"This above all, — to thine own self be true;"

This line is a bit of fatherly advice from Polonius to his son Laertes. Polonius advises his son to stick to what he believes and to not let other people influence his actions or decisions.

Hamlet

"To be or not to be: that is the question:"

This is one of the most famous quotes in English literature. Hamlet feels that life is too painful and complicated. But, he also fears the uncertainty of death. This line has been used in everything from movies to TV shows — Beyoncé Knowles even used it in a song called "Freakum Dress!"

"Sonnet 18"

"Shall I compare thee to a summer's day? / Thou art more lovely and more temperate:"

Many people consider this to be Shakespeare's most famous sonnet. Here, the speaker compares the person he or she loves to a beautiful summer's day. Summer is great, but the object of affection is even better!

temperate: moderate or self-restrained; not extreme

Take Note

For his impressive talent and influence, Shakespeare ranks #1. In his many plays and sonnets, Shakespeare wrote about human nature. Though he was writing more than 400 years ago, his insights still hold true today. Shakespeare's plays are as popular as ever and continue to be performed and adapted. His works have been translated into dozens of languages and have influenced countless writers around the world.

- Read any one of Shakespeare's plays or watch a movie based on his writing. Do you think Shakespeare's work is still relevant today? Give your reasons.

We Thought …

Here are the criteria we used in ranking the 10 most remarkable writers.

The writer:
• Created imaginative works
• Created enduring works
• Is famous around the world
• Expertly expressed certain emotions
• Expertly wrote about a certain time period
• Successfully wrote in more than one genre
• Won awards for his or her work
• Influenced other writers

What Do You Think?

1. Do you agree with our ranking? If you don't, try ranking these writers yourself. Justify your ranking with data from your own research and reasoning. You may refer to our criteria, or you may want to draw up your own list of criteria.

2. Here are three other remarkable writers that we considered but in the end did not include in our top 10 list: Leo Tolstoy, Dante Alighieri, and Miguel de Cervantes.
   - Find out more about these writers. Do you think they should have made our list? Give reasons for your response.
   - Are there other remarkable writers that you think should have made our list? Explain your choices.

Index

A
Alice's Adventures in Wonderland, 15, 17
Alighieri, Dante, 47
And To Think That I Saw It on Mulberry Street, 19
As You Like It, 45
Auden, W. H., 36–37
Austen, Jane, 30–33, 35, 40

B
Becoming Jane, 28
Bellow, Saul, 29
Bloom, Harold, 33, 44
Brattin, Joel J., 24
Bride and Prejudice, 33
Bridget Jones's Diary, 31–32
Byatt, A. S., 16

C
Carrey, Jim, 20, 25
Carroll, Lewis, 14–17, 21
Cat in the Hat, The, 20
Cervantes, Miguel de, 47
Chekhov, Anton, 4
Christmas Carol, A, 24–25
Clueless, 33

D
Dickens, Charles, 22–25
Dickinson, Emily, 38–41
Dr. Seuss, 19

E
Ellison, Ralph, 26–29
Emma, 31, 33

F
Fantasy fiction, 35–37
Fellowship of the Ring, The, 36

G
Geisel, Theodor, 18–21
Great Expectations, 25
Grinch, The, 20

H
Hamlet, 44–45
Harry Potter and the Deathly Hallows, 8–9
Harry Potter and the Philosopher's Stone, 7
Hawke, Ethan, 44
How the Grinch Stole Christmas, 20
Hunting of the Snark, 16

I
I'm nobody! Who are you?, 41
Invisible Man, 26–29

J
Jabberwocky, 16–17
Jackson, Peter, 36–37

K
Kawabata, Yasunari, 12
Kinnell, Galway, 41
Knightley, Keira, 32

L
Lorax, The, 20–21
Lord of the Rings, The, 35–37

M
Mack, Maynard, 44
Mansfield Park, 31
Modernist, 40
Muppet Christmas Carol, The, 25

N
National Book Award, 28
Nobel Prize in Literature, 12
Nonsense fiction, 15–17
Northanger Abbey, 31

O
Oliver!, 25
Oliver Twist, 24–25

P
Persuasion, 31
Pickwick Papers, The, 24
Pride and Prejudice, 31–33
Pulitzer Prize, 20, 29, 41

R
Return of the King, The, 36
Romeo and Juliet, 44
Rowling, J. K., 6–9, 13, 16

S
Seidlitz, Anne, 29
Sense and Sensibility, 31
Shakespeare, William, 42–45
Shikibu, Murasaki, 10–13, 17
Sim, Alastair, 24
Sonnet 18, 45

T
Tale of Genji, The, 11–13
Thomas, James, *8*
Through the Looking-Glass, 15, 17
Tolkien, J. R. R., 34–37
Tolstoy, Leo, 11, 47
Two Towers, The, 36

V
Varadarajan, Tunku, *21*

W
War and Peace, 11